Religion and textual transmission: East India Company sponsored Orientalist scholarship. "Introductions" to the translations of the *Bhagavat Gita* and *Manavadharma*.

Facsimile: A center for early print and society.

Published by

LIES AND BIG FEET

ISBN: 9384281034
ISBN-13: 978-9384281038

THE

BHĂGVĂT-GĒĒTĂ,

OR

DIALOGUES

OF

KRĔĔSHNĂ AND ĂRJŎŎN;

IN EIGHTEEN LECTURES;

WITH

NOTES.

TRANSLATED FROM THE ORIGINAL, IN THE *Sănskrĕĕt*, OR ANCIENT
LANGUAGE OF THE *Brăhmăns*,

BY

CHARLES WILKINS,

SENIOR MERCHANT IN THE SERVICE OF THE HONOURABLE THE EAST INDIA
COMPANY, ON THEIR BENGAL ESTABLISHMENT.

LONDON:
PRINTED FOR C. NOURSE,
OPPOSITE CATHARINE-STREET, IN THE STRAND.
M.DCC.LXXXV.

CONTENTS

THE

BHĀGVĀT-GĒĒTĀ,

OR

DIALOGUES

OF

KRĒĒSHNĀ AND ARJOŎN;

IN EIGHTEEN LECTURES;

WITH

NOTES.

TRANSLATED FROM THE ORIGINAL, IN THE *Sănskrĕĕt*, OR ANCIENT
LANGUAGE OF THE *Brāhmăns*,

BY

CHARLES WILKINS,

SENIOR MERCHANT IN THE SERVICE OF THE HONOURABLE THE EAST INDIA
COMPANY, ON THEIR BENGAL ESTABLISHMENT.

LONDON:
PRINTED FOR C. NOURSE,
OPPOSITE CATHARINE-STREET, IN THE STRAND.
MDCCLXXXV.

PREFATORY NOTE.

This is a collection of primary texts that looks at early colonial-imperial print and the nature of Orientalist scholarship, based on religious texts, that emerged with Sir William Jones, post-1780s. Manuscripts of the Hindu religious texts were often transferred onto print; but what exactly were the processes involved? How did native-brahmins look upon it as they assisted the Britishers in making the shift take place from a manuscript culture to a realm of print technology?

In 1825, Graves Chamney Haughton, a professor of Hindu Literature in the East India College, published an out-of-print text, William Jones's translation of the Sanskrit *Manava Dharma Shastra* or the *Institutes of Manu*. Haughton's prefatory note states that it was a new edition of Sir William Jones's translation; he writes that in his text "the version of the learned translator has been carefully revised and compared" and that discrepancies would have been a result of the "variety of the manuscripts consulted by Sir William Jones."

In 1794, the British government of India had Jones's *Manava Dharma* printed; Sir William Jones, writes in his preface about the processes involved in collaborating with the Brahmins in writing the text:

"…[A]nd the brahman, who read it with me, requested most earnestly, that his name might be concealed; nor would he have read it for any consideration on a forbidden day of the moon,… so great, indeed, is the idea of sanctity annexed to this book, that, when the chief magistrate at Benaras endeavoured, at my request, to procure a Persian translation of it, before I had a hope of being at any time able to understand the original, the Pandits of his court unanimously and positively refused to assist in the work; nor should I have procured it at all, if a wealthy Hindu at Gaya had not caused the version to be made by some of his dependants."

Sir William Jones, operating within the ideology of eighteenth century print culture that associated print with truth, assumed that the technology of print had the power to transform a pre-modern, Indian scribal culture into western modernity. But this equation between print and truth was not intrinsic to letterpress technology as till the early decades of the eighteenth century there was a suspicion of the printed word. In *The Nature of the Book: Print and Knowledge in the Making*, Adrian Johns draws attention to assumptions about print culture, stating that what we "often regard as essential elements and necessary concomitants of print are in fact rather more contingent than generally acknowledged. Veracity in particular is … extrinsic to the press itself, and has had to be grafted onto it."[1] A printed book could never be trusted to be what it claimed. Johns claims that in the seventeenth century,

---

[1] Adrian Johns, *The Nature of the Book: Print and Knowledge in the Making* (Chicago: University of Chicago Press, 2000), p. 2.

piracy and plagiarism were dominant fears. It was a matter

of routine that books could be considered dubious;
therefore, it was impossible to trust any printed report.
Pirate editions of Shakespeare, Donne and Sir Thomas
Browne were liable to egregious errors, and so was Sir Isaac
Newton's unauthorized publication of *Principia* and the first
scientific journal, the *Philosophical Transactions*. It was only in
1760 that the first book was printed without any errors.

The question to ask is thus: did natives operate within a
different parallel epistemic world where multiple
manuscripts of the same text were seen as legitimate;
moreover, why were the brahmins not necessarily keen to
see their names on print, but neither were they hesitant to
transfer a manuscript culture onto print? These early
decades of colonial print can throw more light on the
nature of religious-manuscripts that existed in India, before
the advent of print in India.

SECTION I:
Introduction to the *Bhagavat-Geeta*; translated by Charles Wilkins (1785).[2]

---

[2] *The Bhagavat Geeta, or Dialogues of Kreeshna and Arjoon; in Eighteen Lectures; with Notes.* Translated from the Original, in the Sanskrit, or Ancient Language of the Brahmans, By Charles Wilkins, Senior Merchant, in the Service of the Honourable The East India Company, on their Bengal Establishment. London; Printed for C. Nourse, Opposite Catharine-Street, in the Strand, 1785.

THE

BHĂGVĂT-GĒĒTĀ,

OR

DIALOGUES

OF

KRĔĔSHNĂ AND *ĂRJŎŎN;*

IN EIGHTEEN LECTURES;

WITH

NOTES.

TRANSLATED FROM THE ORIGINAL, IN THE *Sănſkrĕĕt,* OR ANCIENT
LANGUAGE OF THE *Brābmăns,*

BY

CHARLES WILKINS,

SENIOR MERCHANT IN THE SERVICE OF THE HONOURABLE THE EAST INDIA
COMPANY, ON THEIR BENGAL ESTABLISHMENT.

LONDON:
PRINTED FOR C. NOURSE,
OPPOSITE CATHARINE-STREET, IN THE STRAND.

M.DCC.LXXXV.

1 WARRREN HASTINGS INTRODUCTORY COMMENTS.

ADVERTISEMENT.

THE *following Work is published under the authority of the Court of Directors of the East India Company, by the particular desire and recommendation of the Governor General of India; whose letter to the Chairman of the Company will sufficiently explain the motives for its publication, and furnish the best testimony of fidelity, accuracy, and merit of the translator.*

The antiquity of the original, and the veneration in which it hath been held for so many ages, by a very considerable portion of the human race, must render it one of the greatest curiosities ever presented to the literary world.

TO
NATHANIEL SMITH, ESQUIRE.

SIR.

TO you, as to the first member of the first commercial body, not only of the present age, but of all the known generations of mankind, I presume to offer, and to recommend through you, for an offering to the public, a very curious specimen of the Literature, the Mythology, and Morality of the ancient Hindoos. It is an episodical extract from the *Mahabharat*, a most voluminous poem, affirmed to have been written upwards of four thousand years ago, by Kreeshna Dwypayen Veis, a learned Brahmin; to whom is also attributed the compilation of "The Four Vedes, or Bedes," the only existing original scriptures of the religion of Brahma; and the composition of all the Poorans, which are to this day taught in their schools, and venerated as poems of divine inspiration. Among these, and of superior estimation to the rest, is ranked the *Mahabharat*. But if the several books here enumerated be really the productions of their reputed author, which is greatly to be doubted, many arguments may be adduced to ascribe to the same source the invention of the religion itself, as well as its promulgation and he must, at all events, claim the merit of having first reduced the gross and scattered tenets of their former faith

4

into a scientific and allegorical system.

The Mahabharat contains the genealogy and general history of the house of Bhaurut, so called from Bhurrut its founder; the epithet Maha, or Great, being prefixed in token of distinction: but its more particular object is to relate the dissentions and wars of the two great collateral branches of it, called Kooroos and Pandoos; both lineally descended in second degree from Veecheetraveerya, their common ancestor, by their respective fathers Dritarashtra and Pandoo.

The Kooroos, which indeed is sometimes used as a term comprehending the whole family, but most frequently applied as the patronymic of the elder branch alone, are said to have been one hundred in number of whom Dooryodun was esteemed the head and representative even during the life of his father who was incapacitated by blindness. The sons of Pandoo were five; Yudhishteer, Bheem, Arjoon, Nekool, and Sehadeo who, through the artifices of Dooryodun, were banished, by their uncle and guardian Dreetrarashtra, from Hastenapor, at that time the seat of government of Hindostan. The exiles, after a series of adventures, worked up with a wonderful fertility of genius and pompof language into a thousand sublime descriptions, returned with a powerful army to avenge their wrongs, and assert their pretensions to the empire in right of their father; by whom, though the younger brother, it had been held while he lived, on account of the disqualification already mentioned of Dreetrarashtra,

In this state the episode opens, and is called "The Geeta" of "Bhagvat," which is one of the names of Kreeshna. Arjoon is represented as the favorite and pupil of Kreeshna, here taken for God himself, in his last Ootar, or descent to earth in a mortal form.

The Preface of the Translator will render any further explanation of the Work unnecessary. Yet something it may be allowable for me to add respecting my own judgment of a Work which I have thus informally obtruded on your attention, as it is the only ground on which I can defend the liberty which I have taken.

Might I, an unlettered man, venture to prescribe bounds to the latitude of criticism, I should exclude, in estimating the merit of such a production, all rules drawn from the ancient or modern literature of Europe, all references to such sentiments or manners as are become the standards of propriety for opinion and action in our own modes of life, and equally all appeals to our revealed tenets of religion, and moral duty. I should exclude them, as by no means applicable to the language, sentiments, manners, or morality appertaining to a system of society with which we have been for ages unconnected, and of an antiquity preceding even the first efforts of civilization in our own quarter of the globe, which in respect to the general diffusion and common participation of arts and sciences, may be now considered as one community.

I would exact from every reader the allowance of obscurity, absurdity, barbarous habits, and a perverted morality. Where the reverse appears, I would have him receive it(to use a familiar phrase) as so much clear gain, and allow it a merit proportioned to the disappointment of a different expectation.

In effect, without bespeaking this kind of indulgence, I could hardly venture to persist in my recommendation of this production for public notice.

Many passages will be found obscure, many will seem redundant, others will be found clothed with ornaments of fancy unfitted to our taste, and some elevated to a track of sublimity into which our habits of judgment will find it difficult to pursue them; but few which will shock either our religious faith or moral sentiments, something too must be allowed to the subject itself, which is highly metaphysical, to the extreme difficulty of rendering abstract terms by others exactly corresponding with them in another language, to the arbitrary combination of ideas, in words expressing unsubstantial qualities, and more, to the errors of interpretation. The modesty of the Translator would induce him to defend the credit of his work, by laying all its apparent defects to his own charge, under the article last enumerated; but neither does his accuracy merit, nor the work itself require that concession.

It is also to be observed, in illustration of what I have premised, that the Brahmans are enjoined to perform a kind of spiritual discipline, not, I believe, unknown to some of the religious orders of Christians in the Roman Church. This consists in devoting a certain period of time to the contemplation of the Deity, his attributes, and the moral duties of this life. It is required of those who practise this exercise, not only that they divest their minds of all sensual desire, but that their attention be abstracted from every external object, and absorbed, with every sense, in the prescribed subject of their meditation. I myself was once a witness of a man employed in this species of devotion, at the principal temple of Banares. His right hand and arm were enclosed in a loose sleeve or bag of red cloth, within which he passed the beads of his rosary, one after another, through his fingers, repeating with the touch of each (as I was informed) one of the names of God while his mind laboured to catch and dwell on the idea of the quality which appertained to it, and showed the violence of its exertion to attain this purpose by the convulsive movements of all his features, his eyes being at the same time closed, doubtless to assist the abstraction. The importance of this duty cannot be better illustrated, nor stronger marked, than by the last sentence with w hich Kreeshna closes his instruction to Arjoon, and which is properly the conclusion of the Geeta: "Hath what I have been speaking, O Arjoon been heard *with thy mind fixed to one point?* Is the distraction of thought, which arose from thy ignorance, removed?"

To those who have never been accustomed to this separation of the mind from the notices of the senses, it may not be easy to conceive by what means such a power is to be attained; since even the most studious men of our hemisphere will find it difficult so to restrain their attention but that it will wander to some object of present sense or recollection; and even the buzzing of a fly will sometimes have the power to disturb it. But if we are told that there have been men who were successively, for ages past, in the daily habit of abstracted contemplation, begun in the earliest period of youth, and continued in many to the maturity of age, each adding some portion of knowledge to the store accumulated by his predecessors, it is not assuming too much to conclude, that, as the mind ever gathers strength, like the body, by exercise, so in such an exercise it may in each have acquired the faculty to which they aspired and that their collective studies may have led them to the discovery of new tracks and combinations of sentiment, totally different from the doctrines with which the learned of other nations are acquainted, doctrines, which however speculative and subtle, still as they posses the advantage of being derived from a source so free from every adventitious mixture, may be equally founded in truth with the most simple of our own. But as they must differ, yet more than the most abstruse of ours, from the common modes of thinking, so they will require consonant modes of expression, which it may be impossible to render by any of the known terms of science in our language, or even to make them intelligible by definition. This is probably the case with some of the English phrases, as those of "Action," "Application" "Practice," &etc. which occur in Mr. Wilkins's translation, and others, for the reasons which I have recited, he has left with the same sounds in which he found them. When the text is rendered obscure from such causes, candor requires that credit be given to it for some accurate meaning, though we may not be able to discover it; and that we ascribe their obscurity to the incompetency of our own perceptions on so novel an application of them, rather than to the less probable want of perspicuity in the original composition.

With the deductions, or rather qualifications, which I have thus premised, I hesitate not to pronounce the Geeta a performance of great originality; of a sublimity of conception, reasoning, and diction, almost unequalled; and a single exception, among all the known religions of mankind, of a theology accurately corresponding with that of the Christian dispensation, and most powerfully illustrating its fundamental doctrines.

It will not be fair to try its relative worth by a comparison with the original text of the first standards of European composition; but let these be taken even in the most esteemed of their prose translations, and in that equal scale let their merits be weighed. I should not fear to place, in opposition to the best French versions of the most admired passages of the *Iliad* or *Odyssey*, or of the Ist and 6th Books of our own Milton, highly as I venerate the latter, the English translation of the *Mahabharat*.

One blemish will be found in it, which will scarcely fail to make its own impression on every correct mind; and which for that reason I anticipate. I mean, the attempt to describe spiritual existences by terms and image which appertain to corporeal forms. Yet even in this respect it will appear less faulty than other works with which I have placed it in competition; and, defective as it may at first appear, I know not whether a doctrine so elevated above common perception did not require to be introduced by such ideas as were familiar to the mind, to lead it by a gradual advance to the pure and abstract comprehension of the subject. This will seem to have been, whether intentionally or accidentally, the order which is followed by the author of the Geeta; and so far at least he soars far beyond all competitors in this species of composition. Even the frequent recurrence of the same sentiment, in a variety of dress, may have been owing to the same consideration of the extreme intricacy of the subject, and the consequent necessity of trying different kinds of exemplification and argument, to impress it with due conviction of the understanding. Yet I believe it will appear, to an attentive reader, neither deficient in method, nor in perspicuity. On the contrary, I thought it at the first reading, and more so at the second, clear beyond what I could have reasonably expected, in a discussion of points so far removed beyond the reach of the senses, and explained through so foreign a medium.

It now remains to say something of the Translator, Mr. Charles Wilkins. This Gentleman, to whose ingenuity, unaided by models for imitation, and by artists for his direction, your government is indebted for its printing-office, and for many official purposes to which it has been profitably applied, with an extent unknown in Europe, has united to an early and successful attainment of the Persian and Bengal languages, the study of Sanskreet. To this he devoted himself with a perseverance of which there are few examples and with a success which encouraged him to undertake the translation of the

Mahabharat. This book is said to consist of more than one hundred thousand metrical stanzas of which he has at this time translated more than a third; and, if I may trust to the imperfect texts by which I myself have tried a very small portion of it, through the medium of another language, he has rendered it with great accuracy and fidelity. Of its elegance, and the skill with which he has familiarized (if I may so express it) his own native language to so foreign an original, I may not speak, as from the specimen herewith presented, whoever reads it, will judge for himself.

Mr. Wilkins's health having suffered a decline from the fatigues of business, from which his gratuitous labors allowed him no relaxation, he was adviced to try a change of air for his recovery. I myself recommended that of Banares, for the sake of the additional advantage which he might derive from a residence in a place which is considered as the first seminary of Hindoo learning; and I promoted his application to the Board, for their permission to repair thither, without forfeiting his official appointments during the term of his absence.

I have always regarded the encouragement of every species of useful diligence, in the servants of the Company, as a duty appertaining to my office; and have severely regretted that I have possessed such scanty means of exercising it, especially to such as required an exemption from official attendance; there being few emoluments in this service but such as are annexed to official employment, and few offices without employment. Yet I believe I may take it upon me to pronounce, that the service has at no period more abounded with men of cultivated talents, of capacity for business, and liberal knowledge; qualities which reflect the greater lustre on their possessors, by having been the fruit of long and laboured application, at a season of life, and with a license of conduct, more apt to produce dissipation than excite the desire of improvement.

Such studies, independently of their utility, tend, specially when the pursuit of them is general, to diffuse a generosity of sentiment, and a disdain of the meaner occupations of such minds as are left nearer to the state of uncultivated nature; and you, Sir, will believe me, when I assure you, that it is on the virtue, not the ability of their servants, that the Company must rely for the permanency of their dominion.

Nor is the cultivation of language and science, for such are the studies to which I allude, useful only in forming the moral character and habits of service. Every accumulation of knowledge, and especially such as is obtained by social communication with people over whom we exercise a dominion founded on the right of conquest, is useful to the state: it is the gain of humanity: in the specific instance which I have stated, it attracts and conciliates distant affections; it lessens the eight of the chain by which natives are held in subjection; and it imprints on the hearts of our own countrymen the sense and obligation of benevolence. Even in England, this effect of it is greatly wanting. It is not very long since the inhabitants of India were considered by many, as creatures scarce elevated upon the degree of savage life; nor, I fear, is that prejudice yet wholly eradicated, though surely abated. Every instance which brings their real character home to observation will impress us with a more generous sense of feeling for their natural rights, and teach us to estimate them by the measure of our own. But such instances can only be obtained in their writings: and these will survive when the British dominion in India shall have long ceased to exist, and when the sources which it once yielded of wealth and power are lost to remembrance.

If you, Sir, on the perusal of Mr. Wilkin's performance, shall judge it worthy of so honourable a patronage, may I take the further liberty to request that you will be pleased to present it to the Court of Directors, for publication by their authority, and to use your interest to obtain it? Its public reception will be the test of its real merit, and determine Mr. Wilkin's in the prosecution or cessation of his present laborious studies. It may, in the first event, clear the way to a wide and unexplored field of fruitful knowledge; and suggest, to the generosity of his honourable employers, a desire to encourage the first persevering adventurer in a service in which his example will have few followers, and most probable none, if it is to be performed with gratuitous labor of years lost to the provision of future subsistence: for the study of Sanskrit cannot, like the Persian language, be applied to official profit, and improved with the official exercise of it. It can only derive its reward, beyond the breath of fame, in a fixed-endowment. Such has been the fate of his predecessor, Mr. Halhed, whose labors and incomparable genius, in two useful productions, have been crowned with every success that the public estimation could give them; now will it detract from the no less original merit of Mr. Wilkins, that I ascribe to another the title of having led the way, when I add, but the prospect of barren applause. To say more, would be disrespect; and I believe that I address myself to a gentleman who possesses talents congenial with those I am so anxious to encourage, and a mind too liberal to confine its beneficiaries to such arts alone as contribute to the immediate and substantial advantages of the state.

I think it proper to assure you, that the subject of this address, and its design, were equally unknown to the person who is the object of it; from whom I originally obtained the translation for another purpose, which on a second revival of the work I changed, from a belief that it merited a better definition.

A mind rendered susceptible by the daily experience of unmerited reproach, may be excused if it anticipates even unreasonable or improbable objections. This must be my plea for any apparent futility in the following observation. I have seen an extract from a foreign work of great literary credit, in which my name is mentioned, with very undeserved applause, for an attempt to introduce the knowledge of Hindoo literature into the European world, by forcing or corrupting the religious conscience of the Pundits, or professors of their scared doctrines. This reflexion was produced by the publication of Mr. Halhed's translation of the Poottee, or code of Hindoo laws; and is totally devoid of foundation. For myself, I can declare truly, that if the acquisition could not have been obtained but by such means as have been supposed, I should never have sought it. It was contributed both cheerfully and gratuitously, by men of the most respectable characters for sanctity and learning in Bengal, who refused to accept more than the moderate daily subsistence of one rupee each, during the term that they were employed on the compilation; nor will it much redound to my credit, when I add, that they have received no other reward for their meritorius labors. Very natural causes may be ascribed for their reluctance to communicate the mysteries of their learning to strangers, as those to whom they have been for some centuries in subjection, never enquired into them, but to turn their religion into derision, or deduce from them arguments to support the intolerant principles of their own. From our nation they have received a different treatment, and are no less eager to impart their knowledge than we are to receive it. I could say much more in proof of this fact, but that it might look too much like self-commendation.

I have the honor to be,
with respect,

SIR,
Your most obedient
Servant,

WARREN HASTINGS.

P.S. Since the above was written, Mr. Wilkins has transmitted to me a corrected copy of his Translation, with the Preface and Notes much enlarged and improved. In the former, I meet with some complimentary passages which are certainly improper for a work published at my own solicitation. But he is at too great a distance to allow of their being sent back to him for correction, without losing the opportunity, which I am unwilling to lose, of the present dispatch; nor could they be omitted, if I thought myself at liberty to expunge them, without requiring considerable alterations in the context. They must therefore stand; and I hope that this explanation will be admitted as a valid excuse for me in passing them.

W.H.

TO THE HONOURABLE

WARREN HASTINGS,ESQ.

GOVERNOR GENERAL, &C. &C.

HONOURABLE SIR,

UNCONSCIOUS of the liberal purpose for which you intend the Geeta, when at your request, I had the honor to present you with a copy of the manuscript, I was the less solicitous about its imperfections, because I knew that your extensive acquaintance with the customs and religious tenets of the Hindoos would elucidate every passage that was obscure, and I had so often experienced approbation from your partiality, and correction from your pen: It was the theme of a pupil to his preceptor and patron. But since I received your commands to prepare it for the public view, I feel all that anxiety which must be inseperable from one who, for the first time, is about to appear before that awful tribunal; and I should dread the event, were I not convinced that the liberal sentiments expressed in the letter you have done me the honor to write, in recommendation of the work, to the Chairman of the Direction, if permitted to accompany it to the press, would screen me, under its own intrinsic merit, from all censure.

The world, Sir, is so well acquainted with your boundless patronage in general, and of the personal encouragement you have constantly given to my fellow-servants in particular, to render themselves more capable of performing their duty in the various branches of commerce, revenue, and policy, by the study of the languages, with the laws and customs of the natives, that it must deem the first fruit of every genius you have raised a tribute justly due to the source from which it sprang. As that personal encouragement alone first excited emulation in my breast, and urged me to prosecute my particular studies, even beyond the line of pecuniary reward, I humbly request you will permit me, in token of my gratitude, to lay the Geeta, publicly at your feet.

I have the honor to subscribe myself, with great
respect,

Honourable Sir,

Your most obedient, and

Most humble Servant,

Benaras,

19th November, 1784.

CHARLES WILKINS

THE

BHĀGVĀT-GĒĒTĀ,

OR

DIALOGUES

OF

KRĒĒSHNĂ AND ARJŎŎN;

IN EIGHTEEN LECTURES;

WITH

NOTES.

TRANSLATED FROM THE ORIGINAL, IN THE *Sănskrĕĕt*, OR ANCIENT
LANGUAGE OF THE *Brāhmĭns*,

BY

CHARLES WILKINS,

SENIOR MERCHANT IN THE SERVICE OF THE HONOURABLE THE EAST INDIA
COMPANY, ON THEIR BENGAL ESTABLISHMENT.

LONDON:
PRINTED FOR C. NOURSE,
OPPOSITE CATHARINE-STREET, IN THE STRAND.
M.DCC.LXXXV.

THE

BHĂGVĂT-GĒĒTĀ,

OR

DIALOGUES

OF

KRĔĔSHNĂ AND *ĂRJŎŎN*;

IN EIGHTEEN LECTURES;

WITH

NOTES.

TRANSLATED FROM THE ORIGINAL, IN THE *Sănskrĕĕt*, OR ANCIENT
LANGUAGE OF THE *Brāhmăns*;

BY

CHARLES WILKINS,

SENIOR MERCHANT IN THE SERVICE OF THE HONOURABLE THE EAST INDIA
COMPANY, ON THEIR BENGAL ESTABLISHMENT.

LONDON:

PRINTED FOR C. NOURSE,
OPPOSITE CATHARINE-STREET, IN THE STRAND.

MDCCLXXXV.

SECTION II:

Manu's

Manavadharma Shastra.[3]

---

[3] *Manavadharmasastra, or, The Institutes of Manu,* according to the Gloss of Kulluka, comprising the Indian system of Duties, Religious and Civil. Verbally translated from the original, with a Preface by Sir William Jones, and Collated with the Sanskrit Text, by Graves Chanmey Haughton, Esq., Professor of Hindu Literature in the East India College. THIRD EDITION, edited by The Revd. P. Percival, Professor of Vernacular Literature, Presidency College, Madras. (Madras, J. Higginbotham: 1863).

3 INTRODUCTION BY THE REVD. P. PERCIVAL.

D I A L O G U E S

The Professor of Hindu Literature in the East India College, Graves Chamney Haughton, M. A., F.R.S., in the year One Thousand Eight Hundred and Twenty five, published the original Sanskrit text of *Manava Dharma Séstra*, or the *Institutes of Manu*. His beautiful Edition was, by permission, dedicated to the reigning Sovereign of the time. The views which the learned Professor of Haileybury entertained of this ancient record are clearly set forth in his dedication, as may be gathered from the following extract :-

A course of events, unparalleled in the history of mankind, has placed among the subjects of the British Empire, a people renowned from the remotest antiquity, for wisdom, civilization and steadfast adherence to their peculiar religious opinions.

The Institutes of Mann are not only revered by this unvarying race of men, as they were by their primeval forefathers, but have moreover contributed to preserve, in pristine force, opinions, usages and maxims, which by a law, which reverses in the moral, what is observed in the material world, have only grown the stronger by the use of ages.

Although the Editor had to perform the task he took in hand under great disadvantages,——having no native Pundits to consult on the countless nice points of criticism with which he had to deal,——his talent and his rare acquirements enabled him to complete it with great and acknowledged success. His Edition of the original text,—— the result of a careful comparison of nine manuscripts, obtained from various parts of India, with a printed copy executed by Babu Ram, a learned Pundit of Calcutta,——was enriched by critical and explanatory notes. By the unanimous voice of competent judges, Haughton's Edition of the text of Manu has ever been considered as, "one of the most beautiful monuments of true philological research combined with sound criticism that Hindu Literature has to boast of."

More than thirty years before the Edition abovementioned issued from the press, Sir William Jones, justly celebrated for his profound and varied acquirements in different departments of learning, and, more particularly by reason of his great attainments in Oriental Literature, had directed his attention to the Code of Manu. He regarded it as one of the most important records of Hindu antiquity, and therefore resolved, if possible, to prepare an English version for the information of his countrymen. In the attempt to gain an adequate acquaintance with the ancient and sacred Shastra, he had to encounter obstacles almost insuperable. Bigotry and superstition alike opposed him, notwithstanding his high official position. At Benares, the Chief Native Magistrate was unsuccessful in his attempts to procure a Persian translation of the work, the Pundits being unanimous in their refusal to render assistance. The Pundit, with whom Sir William read Sanskrit, reluctantly consented to lend his aid, but only on certain days, when planetary influences were favorable. As preparations for the publication of an English version advanced, the Pundit became alarmed at the prospect of Sir William's success, and apprehending serious consequences to himself, he earnestly requested that his name might in no way appear in connection with the attempt to make known to foreigners the sacred Institutes of the revered Hindu legislator. Eventually a wealthy Hindu at Gaya, caused a version to be made, which assisted Sir William in his design, and enabled him, at an enormous expense of time and labor, to give the result of his endeavours to the European world in an English version. The translation appeared in the, year 1792.

Knowing that the Code was revered by the Hindus as a divine revelation, and universally accepted by them as an unerring guide and directory in all things civil and religious, and consequently the basis on which National Institutions rested, the Government of India ordered an Edition of Sir William's translation to be printed in Calcutta, in a form convenient for reference: it came out of the press in the year 1794.

A new Edition of the version, carefully collated with the original text, was brought out by Professor Haughton in the year 1825. It was printed uniformly with his Edition of the Sanskrit text. The English translation having become exceedingly scarce and dear, it being almost impossible to procure a copy either in London or Calcutta, the publisher determined to bring out a new impression in a cheap and convenient form. There is reason to believe that this new Edition of the Code will be heartily welcomed by all who have a just appreciation of its importance, and especially by those who are brought into contact with Her Majesty's Hindu subjects.

When the Institutes were first made known to Europe, they were carefully studied by oriental scholars and by antiquaries; not perhaps so much on account of their intrinsic value: they were rather appreciated as a literary curiosity, and particularly on account of their antiquity. For practical purposes they were studied only by those whose duties and occupations connected them with India. At that time the extent of British territory was very limited, and the number of public servants but few. And, except as they were represented by the three worthies who were banished from Calcutta to the Danish Settlement of Serampore, and the successors of Ziegenbalg, tolerated likewise by the Danes, on the Coast of Coromandel, teachers of Christian Theology and Western Science had no existence. How wonderfully has the scene changed. The Empire of Britain has, during the short time that has elapsed, been extended to the natural boundaries of the country. Public Servants have been greatly multiplied, and Christian Missionaries, and secular teachers, have been increased a hundred fold. Of late, European capital and enterprise have begun to send forth their Agents to develop the resources, and to share the wealth of the country. Under these altered circumstances a new impression of the Code of Manu must be regarded, not merely as opportune, but as a necessity. To public servants, to those who are engaged in the study and practice of the law, and to Christian teachers, a knowledge of the Institutes must be regarded as indispensable

To public servants, who have to do with the Natives of the country, and to those who are engaged in our Courts of Justice, it must be considered of vital importance to have a correct idea of the principles held sacred by the people whose welfare they are bound to promote. It must not be overlooked that, in all arguments upon the topics of Indian politics, or of judicial amelioration, or of religious instruction, the Legislature of Great Britain has bound itself to act in accordance with those principles which the Hindus firmly believe to have been promulgated originally by the Supreme Being, and which are embodied in the Institutes. However the general public, at Home and in India, may affect to ignore the religious opinions of Her Majesty's Hindu subjects, as of trifling concernment, the servants of the State cannot, thereby, claim exemption from their study and consideration

The scholar will study the Code of Manu because its vast antiquity,—in which it is inferior only to the Vedas,—commends it to him as a literary curiosity; or considering it as a picture of the domestic manners, the politics and the law of a remote age, he may hope to deduce therefrom valuable knowledge more or less of historic value; or he may pore over the singular views that are therein propounded respecting the visible world, and its invisible author, the origin and destiny of the soul, the views given of rewards of punishments, and the doctrine of the metempsychosis. And seeing that the views on these subjects are not those of a people who, like the Chaldees and Egyptians, have perished, but of millions of living beings, our fellow subjects, he cannot fail to cherish an intense interest in the opinions that regulate their conduct in this life, and their belief regarding a future state of being.

It has been frequently said by those who are best acquainted with the Hindus, that every custom prevalent amongst them is based on religion. This is certain. Religion, -- the observance of rites and ceremonies, and of moral and social duties,—is, according to the teachings of the Shastras the final cause of the production of the visible universe. For the various regulations of society and intercourse, marriage and inheritance, birth-rites and funeral pyres, all spring from, and are perpetuated as equally of religious importance. To be convinced of the truth of this, we need only read through the Institutes.

If these things are so, it follows that Christian Missionaries, and indeed all who have to do with the culture of the native mind, whether in matters religious or secular, should acquaint themselves with the sources whence instruction on these points is obtained by the Hindu. However true it may be, that some of the usages it prescribes have, become obsolete, because intended, as some aver, for past and more perfect ages of human existence; and though it may be true, that few are found, especially in Districts in which Sanskrit is little known, that can quote at once an appropriate sloka from the Code in support of their belief or practice, the whole body of Hindus are nevertheless moulded by their great legislator. Those who know them best, and the religious system they venerate, are compelled to believe that the Hindu of today is the same he was in the days of his great legislator. It cannot then be doubted, that those who seek to supersede an anterior system of religion by another, should, as far as practicable, make themselves acquainted with the religious theories of those whom they wish to bring "to the knowledge of the truth." The Christian teacher can no otherwise aim effectually at the opposite party than by knowing exactly the position he occupies, and its defensible strength. Such being the case, Christian teachers should make the Institutes a text book for the study of the system they wish to replace by the introduction of the religion of the Bible. Though Hinduism is found to exist under varied modifications in different sections of the Hindu population, it is essentially one in its source, and that source will be found to be the Code of Manu- The work is short,——a mere tract,—and its chief dogmas and precepts, especially those which form the greatest obstacles to the spread of Christianity, may be easily mastered.

Besides the classes already referred to in these practical remarks, there is another, and a rapidly increasing class, that will, it may be imagined, hail, with great pleasure, the appearance of the sacred ordinances of Hinduism in a new and cheap form. I allude to those who are instructed in the English language. The majority of these, having to devote so large a proportion of their youth to English, and the subjects taught through its medium, can scarcely hope to read the Code of Manu except in a Version. To them this translation must appear of surpassing value. Aided by Sir William Jones' English, the Anglo-Hindu scholar may make himself as perfectly acquainted with the teachings of Manu as if he read them in the Sanskrit, where they are found in their original classic beauty.

In this brief introduction to the present Edition of the Institutes, it is not designed to do more than direct attention to their practical bearing. Their intrinsic quality will be differently estimated by scholars of equal talent and erudition. Some, who have doubtless striven to do justice to the Code, have designated it as, "in some parts, the most worthless, in others, the most precious monument of all Hindu antiquity." The author, but dimly seen amid the mist of a remote antiquity, whoever he was,— whether the son or the grandson of Brahma,—was no doubt profoundly versed in the Vedas: that it contains the principal doctrines and precepts of those early records, is one of its chief excellencies. Apart from all other considerations, "as a picture of ancient manners, in a somewhat advanced state of society, and as a combination of religious precepts and human laws which to a certain extent supply the materials for History," this wonderful book, when rightly studied, will be found replete with valuable knowledge. There is nevertheless much that must prove highly offensive to a refined taste, much needless detail in things exceptionable; there is much also that is high, noble and benevolent.

As indicated in the title page, this Edition is a reprint of Professor Haughton's. The only change introduced, relates to the transliterated words, which have been altered so as to bring them into harmony with the scheme approved by oriental scholars of the present times.

PRESIDENCY COLLEGE

MADRAS,

August 27th, 1863.

P. PERCIVAL.

THE

BHÁGVÁT-GÉÉTÁ,

KRÉÉSHNÁ AND ARJOÖN;

4 INTRODUCTORY COMMENTS TO THE 1825 EDITION, BY G.C. HAUGHTON.

HAVING been for some time engaged in preparing the Institutes of Manu for publication in the Sanskrit language, it appeared to me, that as Sir WILLIAM JONES'S translation had been long out of print, a new edition would not only be acceptable to the public at large, but more especially to those engaged in the study of the Sanskrit language, as the great difficulty of the original text made some help of the kind indispensable. In consequence the version of the learned translator has been carefully revised and compared; and as variations, though of trifling importance, have been discovered, they have been carefully recorded at the end of the work. The discrepancies in question may have arisen from some variety in the readings of the manuscripts consulted by Sir WILLIAM JONES. It appeared, however, advisable to take some notice of those which seemed of most importance to the Sanskrit student. The learned translator intended, as he has stated in his

Preface, to mark by *Italic* letters all that he had borrowed from the Commentators on Manu, and to print the text of his author in *Roman* letters; an arrangement that was intended to afford the reader a precise idea of the original work. It will easily be understood by persons accustomed to the preparation of works for the press, that a rule like this would be occasionally forgotten. And indeed it has sometimes, though rarely, occurred, that passages have been printed in Italic that should have been put in Roman letters. Every attention has therefore been paid to fulfil the translator's intentions, and the reader may be certain that this singularly interesting record of antiquity is now submitted to him with an exactness and fidelity not attained in the former editions. But it is fair to state, that the first and twelfth books are those which are least literal: this is more particularly the case with the latter. The peculiarity of the doctrines contained in these books will account for the fact, and at the same time explain the difficulty the learned translator laboured under in conveying ideas so novel in their nature to the English reader. When, however, the probable antiquity of the original work, and the occasional obscurity of some of its texts, are considered, it must be conceded, that the translator has been generally happy in his interpretation. The great celebrity which has attended the work since its first appearance in England, encourages a hope that its republication will meet the approbation of those, who, though unacquainted with Oriental literature, take an interest in whatever regards the history of the

human mind, and the progress of civilization, to which
European nations are under so many obligations.

G.C. HAUGHTON

East India College, Herts,
6ᵗʰ Jan. 1825.

5 PREFATORY NOTE BY SIR WILLIAM JONES (1794).

PREFACE

BY

SIR WILLIAM JONES

IT is a maxim in the science of legislation and government, that *Laws are of no avail without manners*, or, to explain the sentence more fully, that the best intended legislative provisions would have no beneficial effect even at first, and none at all in a short course of time, unless they were congenial to the disposition and habits, to the religious prejudices, and approved immemorial usages of the people for whom they were enacted; especially if that people universally and sincerely believed, that all their ancient usages and established rules of conduct had the sanction of an actual revelation from heaven; the legislature of Britain having shown, in compliance with this maxim, an intention to leave the natives of these Indian provinces in possession of their own Laws, at least on the titles of contracts and inheritances, we may humbly presume, that all future provisions, for the administration of justice and government in India, will be conformable, as far as the natives are affected by them, to the manners and opinions of the natives themselves; an object, which cannot possibly be attained, until those manners and opinions can be fully and accurately known. These considerations, and a few others more immediately within my province, were my principal motives for wishing to know, and have induced me at length to publish, that system of duties, religious and civil, and of law in all its branches, which the Hindus firmly believe to have been promulgated in the beginning of time by MANU, son or grandson of BRAHMA, or, in plain language, the first of created beings, and not the oldest only, but the holiest, of legislators; a system so comprehensive and so minutely exact, that it may be considered as the Institutes of *Hindu Law*, preparatory to the copious *Digest*, which has lately been compiled by *Pandits* of eminent learning, and introductory perhaps to a Code, which may supply the many natural defects in the old jurisprudence of this country, and, without any deviation from its principles, accommodate it justly to the improvements of a commercial age.

We are lost in an inextricable labyrinth of imaginary astronomical cycles, *Yugas, Mahayugas, Kalpas,* and

Manwantaras, in attempting to calculate the time, when the first MANU, according to the Brahmans, governed this world, and became the progenitor of mankind, who from him are called Manavah; nor can we, so clouded are the old history and chronology of India with tables and allegories, ascertain the precise age, when the work, now presented to the Public, was actually composed; but we are in possession of some evidence, partly extrinsic and partly internal, that it is really one of the oldest compositions existing. From a text of PARASARA, discovered by Mr. DAVIS, it appears, that the vernal equinox had gone back from the *tenth* degree of Brahmani to the *first* of *Aswini,* or *twenty three degrees and twenty minutes,* between the days of that Indian philosopher, and the year of your Lord 499, when it coincided with the origin of the .Hindu ecliptic; so that PARASARA probably flourished near the close of the twelfth century before CHRIST: now PARASARA was the grandson of another sage, named VASISHTA, who is often mentioned in the laws of MANU, and once as contemporary with the divine BHRlGU himself; but the character of BHRIGU, and the whole dramatical arrangement of the book before us, are clearly fictitious and ornamental, with a design, too common among ancient lawgivers, of stamping authority on the work by the introduction of supernatural personages, though VASISHTHA may have lived many generations before the actual writer of it; who names him, indeed, in one or two places, as a philosopher in an earlier period. The style, however, and metre of this work (which there is not the smallest reason to think affectedly obsolete) are widely different from the language and metrical rules of KA'LIDAS, who unquestionably wrote before the beginning of our era; and the dialect of MANU is even observed, in many passages, to resemble that of the Veda, particularly in a departure from the more modern grammatical forms; whence it must at first view seem very probable, that the laws, now brought to light, were considerably older than those of SOLON or even of LYCURGUS, although the promulgation of them, before they were reduced to writing, might have been co-eval with the first monarchies established in Egypt or Asia: but, having had the singular good fortune to procure ancient copies of eleven Upanishads, with a very perspicuous comment, I am enabled to fix with more exactness the probable age of the work before us, and even to limit its highest possible age, by a mode of reasoning, which may be thought new, but will be found, I persuade myself, satisfactory; if the public shall on this occasion give me credit for a few very curious facts, which, though capable of strict proof, can at present be only asserted. The *Sanskrit* of the three first *Vedas* (I need not here speak of the fourth), that of the Manava Dharma Sastra, and that of the Puranas, differ from each other in pretty exact proportion to the Latin of NUMA, from whose laws entire sentences are preserved, that of APPIUS, which we see in the fragments of the Twelve Tables, and that of CICERO, or of LUCRETIUS, where he has not affected an obsolete style: if the several changes, therefore, of Sanskrit and Latin took place, as we may fairly assume, in times very nearly proportional, the Vedas must have been written about 300 years before these Institutes, and about 600 before the *Puranas* and *Itihasa*, which, 1 am fully convinced, were not the production of VYASA; so that, if the son of PARA'SARA committed the traditional Vedas to writing in the Sanskrit of his father's time, the original of this book must have received its present form about 880 years before CHRIST's birth. If the texts, indeed, which VYA'SA collected, had been actually written, in a much older dialect, by the sages preceding him, we must inquire into the greatest possible age of the Vedas themselves: now one of the longest and finest *Upanishads* in the second Veda contains three lists, in a regular series upwards, of at most *forty-two* pupils and preceptors, who successively received and transmitted (probably by oral tradition) the doctrines contained in that *Upanishads*, and as the old *Indian* priests were students at *fifteen*, and instructors at *twenty-five*, we cannot allow more than *ten* years, on an average, for each interval between the respective traditions; whence, as there are *forty* such intervals, in two of the lists, between VYA'SA, who arranged the whole work, and AYA'SA, who is extolled at the beginning of it, and just as many, in the third list, between the compiler and YA'JNYAWALKYA, who makes the principal figure in it, we find the highest age of the *Yajur Veda* to be 1580 years before the birth of our Saviour, (which would make it older than the five books of MOSES) and that of our *Indian* law tract about 1280 years before the same epoch. The former date, however, seems the more probable of the two, because the *Hindu* sages are said to have delivered their knowledge orally, and the very word *Sruta*, which we often see used for the *Veda* itself, means *what was heard*; not to insist, that KULLU'KA expressly declares the sense of the *Veda* to be conveyed in the *language* of VYA'SA. Whether MANU or MANUS in the nominative and MENO'S in an oblique case, was the same personage with MINOS, let others determine; but he must indubitably have been far older than the work, which contains his laws, and, though perhaps he was never in Crete, yet some of his institutions may well have been adopted in that island, whence LYCURGUS, a century or two afterwards, may have imported them to Sparta.

There is certainly a strong resemblance, though obscured and faded by time, between our MANU with his divine Bull, whom he names as DHARMA himself, or the genius of abstract justice, and the MENEUES of Egypt with his companion or symbol, Apia; and, though we should be constantly on our guard against the delusion of etymological conjecture, yet we cannot but admit that MINOS and MNEUES, or Mneuis have only Greek terminations, but that the crude noun is composed of the same radical letters both in Greek and in Sanskrit. "That APIS and MNEUIS," says the Analyst of ancient Mythology, "were both representations of some personage, appears from the testimony of LYCOPHRON and his scholiast; and that personage was the same, who in *Crete* was styled MINOS, and who was also represented under the emblem of the Minotaur DIODORUS, who confines him to Egypt, speaks of him by the title of the bull *Mneuis*,

43

as the first lawgiver, and says, "That he lived after the age of the gods and heroes, when a change was made in the manner of life among men; that he was a man of a most exalted soul, and a great promoter of civil society, which he benefited by his laws; and those laws were unwritten, and received by him from the chief Egyptian deity HERMES, who conferred them on the world as a gift of the highest importance." "He was the same," adds my learned friend, with MENUS, "whom the Egyptians represented as their first king and principal benefactor, who first sacrificed to the gods, and brought about a great change in diet." If MINOS, the son of JUPITER, whom the *Cretans*, from national vanity, might have made a native of their own island, was really the same person with MANU, the son of BRAHMA, we have the good fortune to restore, by means of Indian literature, the most celebrated system of heathen jurisprudence, and this work might have been entitled *The Laws of* MINOS; but the paradox is too singular to be confidently asserted, and the geographical part of the book, with most of the allusions to natural history, must indubitably have been written after the Hindu race had settled to the south of Himalaya. We cannot but remark that the word MANU has no relation whatever to the Moon; and that it was the *seventh*, not the *first*, or that name, whom the Brahmans believe to have been preserved in an ark from the general deluge: him they call the *Child of the Sun*, to distinguish him from our legislator; but they assign to his brother YAMA *the office*(which the Greeks were pleased to confer on MINOS) *of Judge in the shades below.*

The name of MANU is clearly derived (like *menees, mens,* and *mind*) from the root *men to understand* ; and it signifies, as all the Pundits agree, *intelligent,* particularly in the doctrines of the *Veda,* which the composer of our *Dharma Sa'stra* must have studied very diligently; since great numbers of its texts, changed only in a few syllables for the sake of the measure, are interspersed through the work and cited at length in the commentaries: the Public may, therefore, assure themselves, that they now possess a considerable part of the Hindu scripture, without the dullness of its profane ritual or much of its mystical jargon, DA'RA SHUCU'H was persuaded, and not without sound reason, that the first MANU of the Brahmans could be no other person than the progenitor of mankind, to whom *Jews, Christians,* and *Musulmans* unite in giving the name of ADAM; but, whoever he might have been, he is highly honoured by name in the Veda itself, where it is declared, that whatever MANU pronounced, was a medicine for the soul; and the sage VRIHASPATI, now supposed to preside over the planet Jupiter, says in his own law tract, that "MANU held the first rank among legislators, because he had expressed in his code the whole sense of the *Veda*; that no code was approved, which contradicted MANU; that other *Shastras,* and treatises on grammar or logic, retained splendour so long only, as MANU, who taught the way to just wealth, to virtue, and to final happiness, was not seen in competition with them;" VYASA too, the son of PARA'SARA before mentioned, has decided, that the Veda with its *Angas,* or the six compositions deduced from it, the

45

revealed system of medicine, the *Puranas*, or sacred histories, and the code of MANU, were four works of supreme authority, which ought never to be shaken by arguments merely human.

It is the general opinion of Pundits, that BRAHMA taught his laws to MANU in a hundred thousand verses which MANU explained to the primitive world in the very words of the book now translated, where he names himself, after the manner of ancient sages, in the third person; but, in a short preface to the law tract of NA'RAD, it is asserted, that MANU, having written the 'laws of BRAHMA' in a hundred thousand *slokas* or couplets, arranged under *twenty-four* heads in a *thousand* chapters, delivered the work to NA'RAD, the sage among gods, who abridged it, for the use of mankind, in twelve thousand verses, and gave them to a son of BHRIGU, named SUMATI, who, for greater ease to the human race, reduced them to *four thousand*, that mortals read only the second abridgement by SUMATI, while the gods of the lower heaven, and the band of celestial musicians, are engaged in studying the primary code, beginning with the fifth verse, a little varied, of the work now extant on earth; but that nothing remains of NA'RAD's abridgement, except an elegant epitome of the *ninth* original title on the *administration of justice.* Now, since these institutes consist only of *two thousand six hundred and eighty five* verses, they cannot be the whole work ascribed to SUMATI, which is probably distinguished by the name of the *Vridd'ha*, or ancient, *Manava*, and cannot be found entire; though several passages from it, which have been

46

preserved by tradition, are occasionally cited in the new digest.

A number of glosses or comments on MANU were composed by the *Munis*, or old philosophers, whose treatises, together with that before us, constitute the *Dharma Shastra*, in a collective sense, or Body of Law; among the more modern commentaries, that called *Medhatithi*, that by GO'VINDARA'JA, and that by DHARANI'-DHARA, were once in the greatest repute; but the first was reckoned prolix and unequal; the second, concise but obscure; and the third, often erroneous. At length appeared KULLU'KA BHATTA; who, after a painful course of study and the collation of numerous manuscripts, produced a work, of which it may, perhaps, be said very truly, that it is the shortest, yet the most luminous, the least ostentatious, yet the most learned, the deepest, yet the most agreeable, commentary ever composed on any author ancient or modern, European or Asiatic. The Pandits care so little for genuine chronology, that none of them can tell me the age of KULLU'KA, whom they always name with applause; but he informs us himself, that he was a *Brahmin* of the *Varéndra* tribe, whose family had been long settled in *Gaur* or Bengal, but that he had chosen his residence among the learned on the banks of the holy river at Ka'si. His text and interpretation I have almost implicitly followed, though I had myself collated many copies of MANU, and among them a manuscript of a very ancient date: his gloss is here printed in *Italics;* and any reader, who may choose to pass it over as if unprinted, will have in *Roman* letters an exact version of the original, and may form some idea of its character and structure, as well as of the *Sanskrit* idiom, which must necessarily be preserved in a verbal translation; and a translation, not scrupulously verbal, would have been highly improper in a work on so delicate and momentous a subject as private and criminal jurisprudence

Should a series of Brahmans omit, for three generations, the reading of MANU, their sacerdotal class, as all the Pandits assure me, would in strictness be forfeited; but they must explain it only to their pupils of the three highest classes; and the Brahman who read it with me, requested most earnestly, that his name might be concealed; nor would he have read it for any consideration on a forbidden day of the moon, or without the ceremonies prescribed in the second and fourth chapters for a lecture on the Veda: so great, indeed, is the idea of sanctity annexed to this book, that, when the chief native magistrate at Benares endeavoured, at my request, to procure a Persian translation of it, before I had a hope of being at any time able to understand the original, the Pandits of his court unanimously and positively refused to assist in the work; nor should I have procured it at all, if a wealthy Hindu at Gaya had not caused the version to be made by some of his dependants, at the desire of my friend Mr. LAW. The Persian translation of MANU, like all others from the Sanskrit into that language, is a rude intermixture of the text, loosely rendered, with some old or new comment, and often with the crude notions of the translator; and, though it expresses the general sense of the original, yet it swarms with errors, imputable partly to haste, and partly to ignorance: thus where MANU says, *that emissaries are the eyes of a prince*, the Persian phrase makes him ascribe four eyes to the person of a king; for the word *char*, which means *an emissary in Sanskrit*, signifies *four* in the popular dialect.

The work, now presented to the European world, contains abundance of curious matter extremely interesting both to speculative lawyers and antiquaries, with many beauties, which need not be pointed out, and with many blemishes, which cannot be justified or palliated. It is a system of despotism and priestcraft, both indeed limited by law, but artfully conspiring to give mutual support, though with mutual checks; it is filled with strange conceits in metaphysics and natural philosophy, with idle superstitions, and with a scheme of theology most obscurely figurative, and consequently liable to dangerous misconception; it abounds with minute and childish formalities, with ceremonies generally absurd and often ridiculous; the punishments are partial and fanciful; for some crimes, dreadfully cruel, for others reprehensibly slight; and the very morals, though rigid enough on the whole, are in one or two instances (as in the case of light oaths and of pious perjury) unaccountably relaxed: nevertheless, a spirit of sublime devotion, of benevolence to mankind, and of amiable tenderness to all sentient creatures, pervades the whole work; the style of it has a certain austere majesty, that sounds like the language of legislation and extorts a respectful awe; the sentiments of independence on all beings but GOD, and the harsh admonitions even to kings, are truly noble; and the many panegyrics on the *Gayatri,* the *Mother,* as it is called, of the *Veda,* prove the author to have *adored* (not the visible material *sun,* but) *that divine and incomparably greater light,* to use the words of the most venerable text in the *Indian* scripture, which *illumines all, delights all, from which all proceed, to which all must return, and which alone can irradiate* (not our visual organs merely, but our souls and) *our intellects.* Whatever opinion in short may be formed of MANU and his laws, in a country happily enlightened by sound philosophy and the only true revelation, it must be remembered, that those laws are actually revered, as the word of the Most High, by nations of great importance to the political and commercial interests of *Europe,* and particularly by many millions of *Hindu* subjects, whose well directed industry would add largely to the wealth of *Britain,* and who ask no more in return than protection for their persons and places of abode, justice in their temporal concerns, indulgence to the prejudices of their old religion, and the benefit of those laws, which they have been taught to believe sacred, and which alone they can possibly comprehend.

PRINTED FOR C. NOURSE,
OPPOSITE CATHARINE-STREET, IN THE STRAND
MDCCLXXXV.

W. JONES.

THE

BHĂGVĂT-GEETĂ,

OR

DIALOGUES

OF

KRĔĔSHNĂ AND *ĂRJŎŎN*;

IN EIGHTEEN LECTURES;

WITH

NOTES.

TRANSLATED FROM THE ORIGINAL, IN THE *SĂNGSKRĔĔT*, OR ANCIENT
LANGUAGE OF THE *BRĂHMĂNS*,

BY

CHARLES WILKINS,

SENIOR MERCHANT IN THE SERVICE OF THE HONOURABLE THE EAST INDIA
COMPANY, ON THEIR BENGAL ESTABLISHMENT.

LONDON:
PRINTED FOR C. NOURSE,
OPPOSITE CATHARINE-STREET, IN THE STRAND.
MDCCLXXXV.

51

THE

BHĀGVĀT-GEETĀ,

OR

DIALOGUES

OF

KRĒĒSHNĀ AND *ĀRJŌŌN;*

IN EIGHTEEN LECTURES;

WITH

NOTES.

TRANSLATED FROM THE ORIGINAL, IN THE *Sănskrĕĕt*, OR ANCIENT
LANGUAGE OF THE *Brāhmăns*,

BY

CHARLES WILKINS,

SENIOR MERCHANT IN THE SERVICE OF THE HONOURABLE THE EAST INDIA
COMPANY, ON THEIR BENGAL ESTABLISHMENT.

LONDON:
PRINTED FOR C. NOURSE,
OPPOSITE CATHARINE-STREET, IN THE STRAND.
M.DCC.LXXXV.

ABOUT

FACSIMILE: A CENTER FOR EARLY PRINT AND SOCIETY (1780-1820)

Facsimile is an independent research center that works on early print and society in colonial India. It is relevant to remember that print started in Calcutta, India, with the emergence of the East India company in the last two decades of the 18th century.

For more information, please visit us at:

www.colonialprint.wordpress.com

53